AN ANSWER TO DEPRESSION

by

Norman Wright

HARVEST HOUSE PUBLISHERS
Eugene, Oregon 97402

Except where otherwise indicated, Scripture quotations are taken from The Amplified Bible: Old Testament © by Zondervan. The Amplified Bible: New Testament © 1958, The Lockman Foundation. Used by Permission.

An Answer To Depression

© 1976 by Harvest House Publishers,
Eugene, Oregon 97402

Library of Congress Catalog Card Number 76-21111

ISBN 0-89081-059-1

All rights reserved. No portion of this book may be reproduced in any form without the written permission of the publishers.

Printed in the United States of America.

AN ANSWER TO DEPRESSION/1

BEFORE YOU READ THIS BOOK....

1. Write out your own definition of depression.

2. Read over the following statements and whether you agree or disagree with them. If you are using this book with a group, duplicate a copy of the *Agree-Disagree* sheet for each person. Ask the group members to mark in the appropriate space by each statement, and then go through them one-by-one and ask for a show of hands to indicate who agreed and who disagreed. Discuss further those questions which brought a divided response from the group.

2/AN ANSWER TO DEPRESSION

Agree	Disagree	Statement
☐	☐	1. Depression is a sin.
☐	☐	2. Anger can cause a person to be depressed.
☐	☐	3. Jesus experienced a time of depression when He was here on earth.
☐	☐	4. A poor self concept can be the cause of depression.
☐	☐	5. A good way to help a depressed person is to pity him.
☐	☐	6. The Bible teaches that Christians should not be depressed.
☐	☐	7. All depressed people think of suicide.
☐	☐	8. Depression can be a healthy response.

3. If you are working in a group, work together on the following Bible study on people in the Bible who experienced depression. If you are reading this book by yourself, complete the Bible study before you read the book.

MEN IN THE BIBLE WHO EXPERIENCED DEPRESSION

The Men	Extent of the Depression	Causes	God's Solutions
MOSES Numbers 11:10-16 Exodus 18:12-22			
DAVID II Samuel 12:1-17 Psalm 51 Psalm 77			
ELIJAH I Kings 19:1-18			
JONAH Jonah 4:1 ff			

DEPRESSION

For many years you have been a fairly happy and easy going person. You have been conscientious at work and involved in your family. You have had very few physical complaints. But something has changed. You find that you're acting differently. People who know you say, "You're just not yourself anymore." What's going on?

You find it difficult to get out of bed in the morning; if you have any responsibilities for other family members you let them shift for themselves. You're becoming indecisive and even forgetful. Your concentration seems to have fled. You don't feel like laughing, food seems to have lost its taste, and sex has lost its appeal. You might find that you are withdrawing into a shell, not wanting to be bothered by family or friends; and you don't care to talk on the phone or attend social gatherings that you used to enjoy. You're starting to sever all contact with others.

You may have difficulty falling asleep or you may awake in the middle of the night and thrash about until dawn, disturbed by negative and gloomy thoughts. You may want to sleep sixteen hours a day or take frequent naps. But no matter how much you sleep, you still feel exhausted.

Your thoughts are those of hopelessness. There doesn't seem to be any way out of your circumstances. You feel that no one cares for you, and you don't particularly care for yourself. Any positive feelings about yourself have long since gone. You feel as though there were a dark thunder cloud hanging above your head and following you wherever you go.

Physically you may note some changes. You have a number of new vague pains or aches; you may be convinced that you have some serious disease.

There are many other indications, but if you are experiencing the symptoms just described, or you have ever experienced them, then you know what it is to be depressed. If you have never experienced depression in any degree (and you are a rarity) remember that depression is painful for the one who experiences it and at times for the loved ones around the affected person.

How widespread is depression? how normal is it to be depressed? Who gets depressed? Are some people depression prone? What should you do when you get depressed? What causes it? What can you do when your spouse or child begins to get depressed? Do all depressed persons think about suicide? Is it a sin to be depressed?

THESE ARE THE QUESTIONS THAT ARE MOST FREQUENTLY ASKED: THEY MUST BE GIVEN AN ANSWER.

Emotional depression is probably the most common symptom in our country today. Some have said that if the fifties were the age of anxiety the seventies are the age of melancholy or depression. The number of cases of depression has risen to the level of a national epidemic. One out of every eight Americans can be expected to require treatment for depression in his lifetime. In any one year it is estimated that between four and eight million are depressed to the extent that they cannot effectively function at their jobs or they must seek some kind of treatment.

Is depression the cause for the higher rates of suicide in America today? Well, not all depressed people get to the point where they are suicidal. Depression can cover a very broad spectrum, ranging from brief periods of moodiness to long-lasting chronic periods of total despair. Deep, long-lasting, chronic depression may very well result in suicide. Suicide now ranks as the fifth largest killer in the fifteen to fifty-five age group. Dr. Bertram Brown, director of the National Institute of Mental Health, has stated that of those who have clearly committed suicide it is found that over 80 percent of them were definitely depressed. One of the most common things that occurs prior to suicide is depression.[1]

At some time in our lives depression affects each of us. No one is immune, not even the Christian. Some will experience it on a shallow level while others dive to the depths of despondency. The Psalmists reflected these deep feelings of sorrow. "The Lord is close to those who are of a broken heart, and saves such as are crushed with sorrow for sin and are humbly and thoroughly penitent." (Psalm 34:18) And "O Lord, the God of my salvation, I have cried to You for help by day; at night I am in Your presence. Let my prayer come before You and enter into Your presence; incline Your ear to my cry! For I am full of troubles, and my life draws near to the realm of the dead. I am counted among those who go down into the pit (the grave); I am as a man who has no help or strength—a mere shadow; Cast away

---

[1] "What You Should Know About Depression," U.S. News World Report; September 9, 1974

among the dead, like the slain that lie in a (nameless) grave, whom You (seriously) remember no more, and they are cut off from Your hand. (Psalm 88:1-5)

Writers in ancient times described depression as melancholia. The first clinical description of melancholia was made by Hippocrates in the fourth century B. C. He also referred to swings similar to mania and depression (Jelliffe, 1921).

Aretaeus, a physician living in the second century, A.D., described the melancholic patient as "sad, dismayed, sleepless . . . They become thin by their agitation and loss of refreshing sleep . . . At a more advanced state, they complain of a thousand futilities and desire death."

Plutarch, in the second century A.D., presented a particularly vivid and detailed account of melancholia:

> He looks on himself as a man whom the gods hate and pursue with their anger. A far worse lot is before him; he dares not employ any means of averting or of remedying the evil, lest he be found fighting against the gods. The physician, the consoling friend, are driven away. "Leave me," says the wretched man, "me, the impious, the accursed, hated of

the gods, to suffer my punishment." He sits out of doors, wrapped in sackcloth or in filthy rags. Ever and anon he rolls himself, naked, in the dirt confessing about this and that sin. He has eaten or drunk something wrong. He has gone some way or other which the Divine Being did not approve of. The festivals in honor of the gods give no pleasure to him but fill him rather with fear or a fright (quoted by Zilboorg 1941).[2]

WHO GETS DEPRESSED?

Depression affects everyone—both sexes, people of all ages, and the rich and the poor. Just because a person is successful does not protect a person from the possibility of depression. Nor are certain types more prone to depression than others. Artists, movie stars, politicians, people who are in the public spotlight, creative and sensitive people, high achievers, and celebrities are no

---

2. *The Christian Use of Emotional Power*, H. Norman Wright, Fleming H. Revell; Old Tappan, New Jersey, 1976, p. 76.

more depression-prone than others. These people are just more visible than others; if depression hits, the whole world seems to know about it.

One type of person who may be a bit more vulnerable to depression than most is the one who has experienced nothing but success from early childhood. One who has never tasted of defeat may crumble at the first setback.

Are women more prone to depression than men? Women are treated for depression two or three times as often as men. But this evidence is based upon visits to clinics; and clinics are mostly open in the daytime when men are at work. Also, our society traditionally allows women to admit weaknesses or problems and to seek help, but insists that men maintain stability and put up a brave front. Unfortunately males in our culture have been taught not to admit weakness and not to reveal inner feelings. It is interesting to note that male alcoholics outnumber female alcoholics significantly; and the rate for successful suicides is three times higher for men than for women. Men perhaps deal with their depression differently than women do.

Ninety-five percent of even the severely depressed can be totally cured—if the condition is identified early enough. And the everyday, minor depressive episodes can certainly be overcome. But it is important to heed the *early* warning signs of depression and act immediately.

Many have asked "How long does a bout of real depression actually last?" Dr. Aron Beck of the University of Pennsylvania has said that an episode of depression usually "bottoms out" within three weeks; after that the person begins to improve. But unless the problem is diagnosed and help is sought, either from family members or a physician or a counselor, the depression could become worse than it has to. Dr. Floyd Estess of Stanford University Medical School Psychiatry Clinic has estimated that a person with one untreated attack of depression runs a 50-50 risk of a second attack within three years.[3]

---

3. "When the Blues Really Get You Down", Better Homes and Gardens; January, '74.

FEELING DEPRESSED IS LIKE...

Let's examine in detail what it is like to be depressed. Here are ten of the most common characteristics of depression.

1. A person experiences a general over-all feeling of hopelessness, despair, sadness and apathy. It is a feeling of over-all gloom.
2. When a person is depressed he loses perspective. The way you experience your life, your job, your family is colored when you are depressed. As one man said, "There's a real difference between being unhappy and being depressed. When my wife and I have an occasional argument, I'm unhappy about it. I don't like it. But it's part of living. We make up in a fairly short time. I may be concerned over it, but I can sleep all right, and I still feel in good spirits. But when I'm depressed, that's a different matter. It hurts all over; it's almost something physical. I can't get to sleep at night, and I can't sleep through the night. Even though there are still times when I'm in pretty good spirits, the mood comes over me nearly every day. It colors the way I look at everything. If my wife and I have a fight our marriage seems hopeless. If I have a business

problem, which I would normally react to with some tension and frustration but which I deal with promptly and appropriately, I feel as though I'm a lousy businessman and I battle with the problems of self-confidence instead of dealing with the issues in front of me."[4]

3. The depressed person experiences changes in physical activities—eating, sleeping, sex. Sexual interest wanes, and some men find that they cannot perform. This reinforces their feelings of worthlessness. A lessening of sexual interest should always raise the question of depression. Some lose interest in food, whereas others attempt to set a world record at gorging themselves. Some sleep constantly, while others cannot sleep.
4. There is a general loss of self-esteem. The person feels less and less positive about himself and questions his own personal value. Self-confidence is at an all time low.
5. There is a withdrawal from others because of a groundless fear of being rejected. Unfortunately the depressed person's behavior could bring on some rejection from others. The depressed

---

4. *The Secret Strength of Depression*, Frederic F. Flach; J. B. Lippincott Company, New York, '74, p. 15.

person cancels favorite activities, fails to return phone calls, and seeks ways to avoid talking with or seeing others.
6. There is a desire to escape from problems and even from life itself. Thoughts of leaving the home or running away as well as the avoidance of others enters in. Suicidal thoughts and wishes enter because of the feeling that life is hopeless and worthless.
7. A depressed person is oversensitive to what others say and do. He may misinterpret actions and comments in a negative vein and become irritable because of these mistaken perceptions. Often the person cries easily because of misinterpretations.
8. The person has difficulty in handling most of his feelings—especially anger. Anger can be misdirected toward oneself and others. The anger at oneself is based upon feelings of worthlessness and a lack of knowing how to deal with the situation; often this anger is directed outward.
9. Guilt is usually present at a time of depression. The basis for the guilt may be real or imagined. Frequently guilt feelings arise from the assumption that the depressed person is in the wrong somehow or that he is responsible for making

others miserable because of the depression.
10. Often depression leads to a state of dependence upon other people. This reinforces feelings of helplessness; then the person becomes angry at his own helplessness.

IT IS IMPORTANT TO REMEMBER THAT ONCE A PERSON STARTS BECOMING DEPRESSED, HE USUALLY BEHAVES IN A WAY THAT REINFORCES THE DEPRESSION. Read back over the above description of depression and you will begin to note how this happens.

DEPRESSION AND SIN

ONE OF THE QUESTIONS MOST FREQUENTLY ASKED BY CHRISTIANS IS *"Should a Christian ever be depressed? Is depression a sin? Is it usually the result of sin?"*

You may be surprised at the answer that you read here! Depression is basically a sign or symptom of some other disturbance occurring in a person's life. In fact the only healthy reaction to many life situations is depression. Becoming depressed is a common psycho-biological response to stress. We cope with the stresses of life on both a physical and a psychological level; every thought and feeling can produce a change in the chemistry of the nervous system. When we look at the numerous causes for depression you will see the extent of this relationship.

Dr. Frederik Flach has suggested that most people in our society are very well defended against knowing themselves. And any event or change in a person's life that forces him to break any of his defenses can be painful. To experience acute depression can be an opportunity for a person to learn more about himself and also to become more whole than he was before.

Dr. Theodore Rubin has stated that being depressed is a signal that a change is indicated. This can be one of the most constructive times in a person's life if he responds to the signals. It can clear the air and help a person rid himself of years of accumulated anger and hurt. By doing this the depressed person can move toward feeling warmth and love, and can re-evaluate his expectations of life, of himself, and of others.[5]

Unfortunately, we are often threatened by our own depression; we wonder whether we have been sinning or have failed the Lord in some manner. We are also threatened by depression in another believer especially if it is our own spouse. It is difficult to know how to respond to the depressed person. Instead of responding to depression as a signal and finding the cause, we find it tempting to tell the person to "snap out of it" or, "A true Christian doesn't get depressed"; or we say or think; "Didn't you know that being depressed is a sin?" If you were depressed and someone said that to you how would you feel? Would you get better or would you go deeper into your despondency?

Unfortunately many of us have heard pastors preach that being depressed is a sin in and of itself. Every time I hear that I cringe, for I hurt for the people in the congregation who may be depressed. I wonder what that sort of message does to them.

Christians do get depressed, and depression IS NOT A SIN. One of the causes for

---

[5]. "Psychiatrist's Notebook", Dr. Theodore Rubin; Ladies Home Journal; May '76, p. 26.

depression may be sin, but the state of depression itself is not a sin. In many cases depression is the healthiest response to what a person is doing to his life. Depression is a normal reaction to what is happening to him psychologically and physically. Depression is a scream, a message to him that he has neglected some area of his life. He should listen to his depression, for it is telling him something that he needs to know. *Depression is a signal that something in his life is not right*; he ought to respond to the message.

Often in counseling a person experiencing depression I will ask, "Is there any way that you could thank God for being depressed?" Often the response is a puzzled look. Their depression hurts; a person wonders what I mean by thanking God for it. I might say, "Perhaps it is possible to thank God for your depression because it is a signal that some other area of your life is crying out for recognition and help. If you weren't depressed you could be in even worse shape!"

We need to see depression as a message; we need to respond to that message as soon as we can. As we look at the many causes for depression we will see how this is true. We will also note several people in the scriptures who experienced depression, and, we will explore what it meant in their lives.

CAUSES OF DEPRESSION

What are the various causes of depression? Isn't sin the main one?

When one thinks of depression it is important to distinguish between the various kinds that plague people. Such a simple thing as not eating properly or not getting proper rest can cause depression. The person who does not eat regular meals or get sufficient sleep may find himself becoming depressed because he is cheating his body of the food and rest it needs to keep functioning properly. College students often suffer from this type of depression. The cure is simple and obvious: eat right and get enough sleep.[6] This principle is in keeping with the scriptural teaching that the believer's body is the temple of the Holy Spirit. Eating the right type of food and eating it regularly honors the Spirit by properly maintaining His dwelling place. This is fitting in light of our call to present our bodies to Him: "I appeal to you therefore, brethren, and beg of

---

6. *The Christian Use of Emotional Power*, p. 77.

you in view of (all) the mercies of God, to make a decisive dedication of your bodies—presenting all your members and faculties—as a living sacrifice, holy (devoted, consecrated) and well pleasing to God, which is your reasonable (rational, intelligent) service and spiritual worship." (Romans 12:1)

Reactions to certain drugs can affect a person's moods. Medications administered to correct a physical disturbance may cause a chemical change in the body that brings on the blues. All drugs affect the body and the mental processes in some way. If a drug results in brain or nervous system toxicity, extreme depression could be the result. If a person takes too much of a drug or sedative over an extended period of time he may be a candidate for toxic depression. The symptoms are listlessness, indifference, and difficulty in concentrating. Often the person evidences odd and illogical thought patterns which interfere with his normally good judgment. In many cases the depression and drug toxicity will clear up in a day or so after the drug is no longer in the system.[7]

A high school girl who came to me for counseling was quite depressed. For several sessions neither of us could determine the

---

7. *The Christian Use of Emotional Power*, p. 78.

cause until she mentioned that she had gone to her medical doctor a few weeks earlier. She complained of irregularity in her menstrual cycle, so the doctor, in order to regulate it, prescribed birth control pills. A week later the depression hit. After we talked about this the girl went back to the doctor; he had her stop taking the pill. Within days the depression lifted. She was one of those who cannot take the birth control pill without side effects.

If a person who is taking any kind of medication, prescribed by a doctor or not, becomes depressed, he should seek his physician's advice and counsel. The doctor may want to change the dosage or the medication. It is unwise to prescribe medication for oneself.

There are many physical causes for depression. Infections of the brain or nervous system, generalized body infections, hepatitis and hypoglycemia can cause depression. Glandular disorders, a low thyroid condition, hyperthyroidism, excessive ovarian hormonal irregularities, and an imbalance of secretions from the adrenal or pituitary glands also cause a type of depression. Usually other symptoms and bodily changes are also in evidence.

Repressed anger turned inward upon

oneself will lead to depression. In fact repressed anger is commonly used as a synonym for depression. This type of anger has been turned from its original source to the inner person. As William Blake wrote in "A Poison Tree":

> I was angry with my friend:
> I told my wrath, my wrath did end.
> I was angry with my foe:
> I told it not, my wrath did grow.[8]

Reactive depression, usually called grief depression, immediately follows the loss of a loved one, a job or some important opportunity. The intensity of this type of depression is greater immediately after the loss and lessens as the weeks go by. During this time the person's usual functions of living may be impaired but he can still operate within normal limits. There is a sense of emptiness because of the loss. For the most part, however, his feelings about himself and his self-esteem remain the same. We expect this type of grief depression when a person loses a loved one or even a close friend. Grief is very important in helping a person regain his full functioning capabil-

---

8. *The Christian Use of Emotional Power*, p. 78-80.

ities.[9] Jesus himself experienced the depth of these feelings when he was in the garden: "And talking with Him Peter and the two sons of Zebedee, He began to show grief and distress of mind and was deeply depressed. Then He said to them, My soul is very sad and deeply grieved, so that I am almost dying of sorrow..." (Matthew 26:37, 38).

Another major type of depression is biochemical or endogenous—generated internally. It is caused by a disturbance in the body's chemical system. Depression results when the brain and part of the nervous system become disorganized and no longer function normally.

Today more and more researchers and writers are emphasizing the role of our thought life in causing depression. Faulty and negative thinking is at the root of much depression. The thinking pattern that will be discussed here is that found in the person who has a low self concept or self image. This low self-esteem leads to depression; then, when the person is depressed, the low self image is reinforced and intensified; and that feeds the depression.

---

9. *The Christian Use of Emotional Power*, p. 84, 85.

THE DEPRESSIVE TRIAD

To best describe the thinking process of a depressed individual consider these three faulty patterns of thought which distort the individual's total view of life. We will call this pattern the *Depressive Triad*.

DEPRESSIVE TRIAD
Thinking Patterns
A Negative View Of

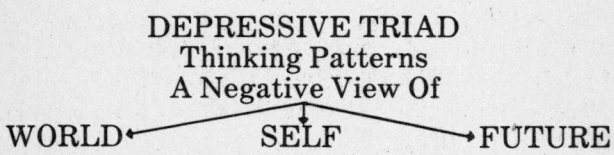

WORLD	SELF	FUTURE
Construes experience in a negative way. Sees defeat, deprivation or disparagement.	Regards self as deficient, inadequate, unworthy. Sees self with a defect—then regards self as undesirable and worthless — then rejects self.	Anticipates that current difficulties will continue. Sees a future life of hardship, frustration and deprivation.

THE RESULTS

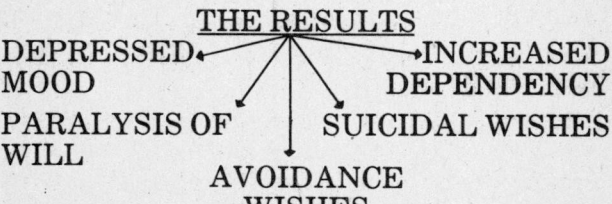

DEPRESSED MOOD

INCREASED DEPENDENCY

PARALYSIS OF WILL

SUICIDAL WISHES

AVOIDANCE WISHES

The first part of the Depressive Triad is concerned with a person looking at his experiences in a negative manner. This gives him a negative view of the world. He interprets (whether right or wrong) his interactions with the world as representing defeat, disparagement, or deprivation. All of life is filled with burdens and obstacles and these detract from the person. NEGATIVE THINKING CAN LEAD A PERSON INTO DEPRESSION. AND WHEN HE IS DEPRESSED HE CONTINUES TO THINK MORE AND MORE NEGATIVELY, WHICH REINFORCES THE DEPRESSION.

The person with a negative view of the world interprets his experiences as actually detracting from himself. Even neutral experiences are interpreted in a negative manner. A neutral attitude on the part of a friend is seen as rejection. A neutral comment is interpreted as a hostile remark. His thinking pattern is clouded by reading into the remarks of others that which fits his previously drawn negative conclusions. He makes assumptions and selective abstractions, generalizes, and magnifies events and remarks way out of proportion. He is so predisposed to negative thinking that he automatically makes negative interpretations of situations. Defeat is his watchword.

MORE CAUSES OF DEPRESSION

Excessive self pity will also lead to depression. In fact, an overabundance of self pity indicates a poor self concept. Most of us have felt sorry for ourselves at one time or another. That is normal; but to wallow in it is an invitation to depression.

Another common cause for depression has to do with our behavior. If the way you are acting is contrary to your moral standards or your value system, depression could be the result. A Christian man who has a high standard of morality but gets involved in an affair could experience depression. A parent who does not live up to his understanding of the scriptural pattern in dealing with his children could wonder why he is depressed; the answer could be in the conflict between the standard and the actual behavior. When behavior is violating scriptural teaching and depression results, then we may honestly say that sin is the cause for the depression.

Had you ever considered that achieving success could bring on depression? It can happen. One who has worked hard and strived for a position finally attains the goal. And much to his amazement he becomes depressed. It could be that all of the emotional and physical energy he exerted has left him depleted. Or it could be that in the new position he feels inadequate and uncertain; the demands for a higher level of performance could be threatening to his confidence and self-esteem. His newly won level of success is not just an achievement, but a new challenge and more work!

The common thread that underlies much of depression is that of loss. Whenever a person experiences a real or an imagined loss, depression may result. That is why in counseling we search to discover if there has been some loss. Many losses are perceived as a threat to security or self esteem, since the object or person lost is viewed as vital for one's existence or day-to-day functioning. It is common for adolescents to undergo bouts of depression as the normal developmental process presents teenagers with many real losses and threats to their self-esteem. They want independence, and yet the loosening of ties to parents and the making of decisions creates anxiety and insecurity.

More and more research is being conducted on how we respond to loss or even change in our lives. In a 1971 issue of *Science Digest* a study by Dr. Eugene S. Pakyel was reported. Three hundred and seventy-three people were asked to rate the events that would be the most "upsetting" in their life.

The twenty-five most distressing events (and those which can induce a depressive reaction) in order of importance, were:

1. Death of a child
2. Death of a spouse
3. A jail sentence
4. An unfaithful spouse
5. Major financial difficulty
6. Business failure
7. Being fired
8. A miscarriage or stillbirth
9. Divorce
10. Marital separation due to an argument
11. A court appearance
12. Unwanted pregnancy
13. A major illness in the family
14. Unemployment for a month. (Additional studies indicated that four out of five marriages end in a divorce when the man is out of work for nine months or more.)
15. Death of a close friend
16. A demotion
17. A major personal illness
18. Start of an extramarital affair
19. Loss of personally valuable objects
20. A lawsuit
21. Academic failure
22. Child married without family approval

23. A broken engagement
24. Taking out a large loan
25. Son drafted

A man might respond to some of these differently than a woman, but these were the most significant events as described by the people in the study. You might discuss these with your family and have each family member make his or her own list. Knowing what distresses a person the most may assist you in responding to him or her in a time of depression.

Both Moses and Elijah give us clear examples of some of the causes of depression. They especially illustrate the type of thinking pattern which is evident in depression.

"And Moses heard the people weeping throughout their families, every man at the door of his tent; and the anger of the Lord blazed hotly, and in the eyes of Moses it was evil. And Moses said to the Lord, Why have You dealt ill with Your servants? And why have I not found favor in Your sight, that You lay the burden of all this people on me? Have I conceived all this people? Have I brought them forth, that You should say to me, Carry them in your bosom, as a nursing father carries the sucking child, to the land which You swore to their fathers (to give them)? Where should I get meat to give to all these people? For they weep before me and say, Give us meat, that we may eat. I am not able to carry all these people alone, because the burden is too heavy for me. And if this is the way You deal with me, kill me, I pray You, at once and be granting me a favor, and let me not see my wretchedness (in the failure of all my efforts)." (Numbers 11: 10-15)

Moses was complaining to the Lord "Why me? Why must I have this burden?" He actually believed that he was carrying the burden himself; at the same time he was reflecting his feelings of inferiority (see vs. 14, and 15). It is interesting that men can be reluctant to relinquish tasks or authority to others even though the amount of work they place upon themselves is unbearable. Then because of this inability to delegate, everything looms out of perspective. God dealt with Moses in a very simple manner—He divided up the labor among the elders of Israel. There are times when we wouldn't have to experience depression if we would quit attempting to do it all ourselves and would call for help.

Elijah is a classic example of the tortures of depression. Elijah's despondency moved him to the point of wanting to die. (Read the account in I Kings 18, 19.) Elijah is an example of a man who misinterpreted a situation and saw only certain elements of it. He had misconceptions concerning himself, God and others. This happened partly because of his tremendous emotional and physical exhaustion.

Elijah had an intense emotional experience in the demonstration of the power of God. Perhaps he expected that everyone would turn to the true God, and was disappointed when Jezebel was still so hostile. He was physically exhausted because of the encounter on Mt. Carmel and his twenty mile race before the king's chariot. When Jezebel threatened his life he became frightened. He probably spent time dwelling upon the threat (and forgetting about God's power which had just been demonstrated). Fearing for his life, he left familiar surroundings and cut himself off from his friends. All of these factors led to the depression. The distortion of his thinking is evident in his idea that he was the only one left, the only one who was faithful to God. He was convinced that the whole world was against him. Possibly he had some self pity which helped him to lose perspective.

But the graciousness of the Lord is evident

in this account. Nowhere did God berate Elijah for being depressed, or tell him to confess his depression as a sin! Instead He sent an angel to minister to Elijah. The prophet slept and was given food. God allowed Elijah to "get everything off his chest." The prophet told God his complaint and concern. Then God did two things: He pointed out to Elijah the actual reality of the situation; and He asked Elijah to get into action—He gave him an assignment. This account of Elijah helps us see the various causes of depression; it also gives us an insight as to how God responds to a depressed person.

After considering the many things that can cause it, you may feel that depression is a complex condition! Yes, it can be, especially when several of the causes work together to develop the depression. But depression does not have to be the end of the world, even though to the depressed individual it appears that way. There are ways to cope and ways to counteract the causes of depression. This can be an opportunity for change and growth as the causes are pinpointed and steps are taken to rebuild the areas of life that are causing problems.

Is it possible that some people gain a benefit from depression and don't want to give it up?

Yes. A housewife might use her depression, even though it hurts, to gain attention and sympathy from her husband. If she notices an increase in attentiveness during her bouts of depression, she might tend to resist giving up the depression. She may feel that the pain of depression is worthwhile because of her husband's response. A husband may avoid taking responsibility in the family by being depressed.

A salesman came to me for counseling because of extensive depression. He hadn't made a sale in six weeks; when he arrived at the office each morning, instead of making thirty or so phone calls, as he usually did, he would sit there staring at the wall and sensing his depression. Then he would go home for the night and still be depressed. The next morning the same pattern was repeated. One day he admitted that in a sense he liked his depression because it numbed him to the pain of not making any sales, and he could also use the depression as an excuse for not making any sales.

A housewife admitted in counseling that she felt her depression was her way of getting back at her husband for being such a rotten person. She seemed to enjoy the pain and upset her depression caused him. This newly discovered weapon was so effective that she was hesitant to give it up.

THE DEPRESSING ENVIRONMENT

I realize that a person is responsible for his own emotions, but can one family member cause depression in another? Could a person help to create an environment that would tend to bring on depression?

Yes, it is possible to create what is called a depressogenic environment. This type of environment is contrary to the teaching of the Scripture that all believers are members of the body of Christ. As believers we are to encourage, to edify and to build up one another. We have been called to love one another. Especially in the marriage relationship, love is to be a sacrificial, servanthood type of love.

A depressogenic environment is one that does not provide a person with adequate support for his self-esteem. In most cases this environment undermines self-esteem or elicits emotions and conflicts that the person cannot handle just then without becoming depressed. Constant attack by someone whom we love and respect can bring on feelings of hurt, guilt and helplessness which can lead to depression. Colossians 3:21 states: "Fathers, do not provoke or irritate or fret your children—do not be hard on them or harass them; lest they become discouraged and sullen and morose and feel inferior and frustrated; do not break their spirit." Proverbs 11:29 (TLB): "The fool who provokes his family to anger and resentment will finally have nothing worthwhile left. He shall be the servant of a wiser man."

In this depressogenic environment the thousands of negative verbal and nonverbal exchanges can affect the vulnerable person. We are not saying that the depressed person is not responsible for his depression but the environment without support can get the process started. Some people are more vulnerable than others to such an environment.

The tactics most commonly employed in families to induce depression are identified on the list that follows. Use this list to evaluate the atmosphere of your own home. If any of these are present take steps immediately to correct them. This could be done by confronting family members with their actions; talking to a friend, pastor, or counselor; or getting books and other resources to help counteract depressogenic behaviors.

Without being facetious, then, here are the ten best ways to help a family member become depressed:

1. Try to control the other person so he cannot gain any type of independence. The control may be subtle or overt, but you direct his life for him. Eventually this leads him to believe that he cannot exist without your direction.
2. Try to convince the other person that he needs you and could not survive without your emotional support.
3. Give your spouse or child ambivalent messages that undermine self-esteem, such as, "In spite of how sloppy you are, I still love you," or, "I guess this is just the burden that I have to bear, having a child (or a husband) like you. But I still do care for you."
4. Try to provoke guilt by making the other person feel responsible for situations or conditions. Make him feel miserable. This can be done without ever saying a word.

A housewife once reflected how she felt when her husband would come home and, without saying a word, would look around the house to see if it were clean, and then would cast a disgusted look her way. She was a neat housekeeper, but he was a perfectionist. With a look and with silence the rest of the evening he successfully conveyed to her his annoyance.

5. Misinterpret the person's intentions and motives so he begins to doubt his own perceptions. This can be done by constantly questioning: "Are you sure you did that or said that?" or, "I don't think anyone else heard you say that . . ." or, "You don't really mean that—you're just saying it because . . ." After a while the person may begin to doubt himself.

6. Make sure the communication process is blocked. This is the surest way to reject a person and also to build indifference in a relationship. Remain silent, or just respond on a cliche level with no deep feeling. Creating an atmosphere where people cannot express true feelings or ideas is the way to destroy a relationship.

7. Insert a competitiveness into the family relationships. Anything that can be done to build envy and jealousy will have a detrimental effect upon the family. Com-

paring one child with another, or giving more attention to one child to get back at your spouse.
8. Maintain a monotonous environment without any joy or humor. As people share funny experiences or their delight in events, and they receive no positive response they begin to wonder about themselves; eventually they will quit sharing.
9. Refuse any show of emotions, especially healthy reactions of anger. Do not allow the other family members to express their emotions. As they learn to bottle up their anger, one of the best outlets or channels for it will be depression.
10. Become depressed yourself to express some indirect anger toward the other person. Try to make him feel confused and helpless.[10]

As you can see, the items on the list do nothing to build confidence and self-esteem. And yet these conditions exist in many homes. People ask, "Why are people so depressed in our home?" If you found that you identified with all or part of the list, please talk over your situation with other

---

10. Adapted from Flach.

family members. Take the necessary steps to build a healthy atmosphere in your home in which it would be difficult to become depressed because of the environment.

WHAT TO DO ABOUT DEPRESSION

If I find that I am becoming or I am already depressed what can I do about it? Should I let my husband or wife know?

Let's talk about what you can do if you find yourself becoming depressed. First of all check for any physical reasons for your depression. You may even want to see your medical doctor. If there is no physical cause, then your next step is to ask yourself two key questions. It's perfectly in order to ask your mate or a good friend to assist you as you think about the questions:

1. What am I *doing* that might be bringing on my depression? (Check your behavior to determine that it is consistent with scripture. Ask yourself if you are doing anything to reinforce the depression).
2. What am I *thinking* about or in what way am I thinking that might be making me depressed?

If your thinking pattern is negative and you persist in making negative value judgments about yourself, you can break this pattern. First, recognize and identify the thoughts that you express to yourself. When something happens and you experience depression, you need to realize that there is more than the outward occurrence behind your feelings. Perhaps you had a negative thought or made a negative value judgment regarding the thing that happened. This sets you up for depression. Second, realize that many of your thoughts are automatic. They are involuntary. You don't have to think about having them, they just pop in. They are not the result of deliberation or reasoning. But if you do reason against them you can put them aside.

Third, distinguish between ideas and facts. You may *think* something, but that does not mean that it is true. If you feel that your spouse does not like the way you dress or the meals you cook, check it out with him. You may be right, but you could also be wrong. If you make an assumption always try to verify it and see if it is true.

Finally, after you have discovered that a particular thought is not true, state precisely why it is inaccurate or invalid. This step is vital! Putting the reasons into words helps you in three ways: it actually reduces the frequency of the ideas coming back; it decreases the intensity of the idea; and it tones down the feeling or mood that the idea generates. The more you counteract some of your ideas in this manner the more your depression is lessened.

Watch any assumptions or generalization that you make. Learn to say to yourself, "I'm jumping to a conclusion again," or "I exaggerated again," or "I assumed that she didn't like it—but it could just as well be true that she liked it." Strange as it seems, it is important for you (when you are alone of course) to do this aloud; you need to hear your own voice expressing this idea. Remember, your thinking pattern can be changed.

11 Timothy 1:7: "For God did not give us a spirit of timidity—of cowardice, of craven and cringing and fawning fear—but (He has given us a spirit) of power and of love and of calm and well-balanced mind and discipline and self-control."

Ephesians 4:23: "And be constantly renewed in the spirit of your mind—having a fresh mental and spiritual attitude."

11 Peter 1:13: "I think it right, as long as I am in this tabernacle (tent, body), to stir you up by way of rememberance."

We are called upon to change our thinking pattern or our thought life; but the scripture also states (Rom. 12:2, Eph. 4:23) that the Holy Spirit is actively at work in influencing our mind and helping us to control our thoughts.

Here are two suggestions that have helped many people to correct their thought life from a negative pattern to a positive. A physician asked a patient to keep a stopwatch with him and to click it on whenever he had a negative thought and to click it off when a positive thought came in to replace it. He noted the blocks of time on a sheet of graph paper, and carried the watch and the paper with him wherever he went. Before this experiment, he felt that the negative thoughts were in his mind constantly. By timing them and putting them on a graph he found that they did not occur as often as he thought. The whole process of timing the thoughts helped him to develop methods of controlling the negative thoughts he did have. He began to take control of his life again.

Another method of breaking a negative thinking pattern involves writing Phillipians 4:6-9 "Do not fret or have any anxiety about anything, but in every circumstance and in everything by prayer and petition (definite requests) with thanksgiving continue to make your wants known to God.", on a 4 x 6-inch card; on the other side of the card writing the word "STOP" in large letters. Any time a negative or worrisome thought comes into your mind take out the card. If you are alone, look at the card and say the word "STOP" out loud. Then turn the card over and say the scripture out loud. If you are at work or with others you may read silently. Do this regularly, and you will defeat the negative thought pattern and replace it with the positive thoughts of the Scripture.

The following checklist suggests some questions to ask yourself and some additional ways of dealing with your depression.

QUESTIONS TO ASK AND STEPS TO TAKE IN OVERCOMING DEPRESSION:

1. What is my depression doing for me? Am I getting anything out of being depressed?
2. Have I undergone any major changes or stresses during the past few months or years? What are they? How am I trying to adjust to them?
3. What kind of environment am I in? Is it helping me to come out of my depression, or could it be making me more depressed?

4. Look at your eating and sleeping habits to see if these ought to be changed.
5. Are you following your normal routine of life or are you withdrawing by staying in bed longer, staying away from friends, letting the dishes stack up in the sink, avoiding regular activities? Are you cutting yourself off from your friends and family? If so, it is important to force yourself to stay active, as hard as it might seem. Remember that a depressed person begins behaving and acting in such a way that the depression is reinforced. You must break the depressive pattern of behavior by yourself or by asking someone to help you.
6. Let your mate know that you are depressed. Ask him to listen to you as you explain it. If you want him to comment, let him do so; but if not, tell him you'd rather he didn't. If you are angry with him, or with anyone, discuss your feelings with them and get it out into the open.
7. Each day, either by yourself or with another's help, make a list of what you would do during that day if you were not depressed. After you have made this list in detail, work out a plan whereby you will follow what is on that list each day.

Another way of developing a pattern of

positive behavior is to make an extensive list (with the help of others) of Pleasant Events. After the list is made, select several to do each day. This Pleasant Events schedule is not a panacea for all depression; but often you can break the pattern of depression through your behavior. Most people feel better when they engage in pleasant activities.
8. Be sure to read the books suggested in the study portion of this book. These will assist you in developing a thinking pattern that could lift the depression. Focusing and dwelling upon positive scriptures will also help you. Each morning read these passages; put them on posters and place them around the house: Psalm 27:1-3; 37:1-7; Isaiah 26:3; and Isaiah 40:28-31.

WHERE IS GOD?

Isaiah 43:1-3 says, "But now (in spite of the past judgments for Israel's sins) thus says the Lord Who created you, O Jacob, and He Who formed You, O Israel: Fear not, for I have redeemed you—ransomed you by paying a price instead of leaving you captives; I have called you by your name, you are Mine. When you pass through the waters I will be with you, and through the rivers they shall not overwhelm you; when you walk through the fire you shall not be burned or scorched, nor shall the flame kindle upon you. For I am the Lord your God, the Holy One of Israel, your Savior; I give Egypt (to the Babylonians) for your ransom, Ethiopia and Seba (a province of Ethiopia) in exchange for your release." This scripture is very comforting and at the same time deals with a misconception that believers often hold. Many feel that being a Christian is an insurance policy against everyday difficulties and emotional problems. This verse does not say that we will go around or above the fire or water but that as we go *through* it God is with us! In the midst of difficulty it is possible to learn peace and contentment.

Elizabeth Skoglund in her book *The Whole Christian* says, "Many Christians seem to think that they are always to be the opposite of depressed, that is, happy and joyful. The rightness or wrongness of that viewpoint lies in one's definition of those words. A light sort of continued 'up' feeling is not, in my opinion, what God expects of us; and to teach that this is a necessary characteristic of a good Christian is to cause great discouragement and guilt. What God does give to a

Christian is a settled sense of contentment. One person who has suffered greatly said with tears: 'I am glad God has used my pain to bring something good into this world, and if I could choose to change it all and lose the good, I would not change even the pain. But I did not like the pain nor do I like it now.' She was content but not masochistically happy over suffering. At times she had been depressed and frightened, but never had she lost that deep sense of God's control and strength in her life. Such an attitude reminds one of Paul's words: 'We are troubled on every side, yet not distressed; we are perplexed, but not in despair; persecuted, but not forsaken; cast down, but not destroyed." (II Cor. 4:8, 9 KJV)[11]

A depressed person might read this account and say, "But that's not me. I'm not like that" and begin to feel worse. Remember, it is a process to arrive at that point. It does not happen overnight. But it is possible! When you are depression-prone you need to develope a sense of God's great love for you. The following paraphrase of I Corinthians 13, titled "Because God Loves Me," will help you "tune-in" to God's love. Read the paraphrase *out loud* every morning and evening.

---

11. *The Whole Christian*, Elizabeth R. Skoglund; Harper & Row, New York, '76, p. 12.

Concentrate on the words. Read with meaning and emphasis. As you hear your own voice stating the facts about God's love, gradually the realization of that love will seep into your life.

BECAUSE GOD LOVES ME
I Cor. 13:4-8

Because God loves me He is slow to lose patience with me.

Because God loves me He takes the circumstances of my life and uses them in a constructive way for my growth.

Because God loves me He does not treat me as an object to be possessed and manipulated.

Because God loves me He has no need to impress me with how great and powerful He is because *He is God* nor does He belittle me as His child in order to show me how important He is.

Because God loves me He is for me. He wants to see me mature and develop in His love.

Because God loves me He does not send down His wrath on every little mistake I make of which there are many.

- Because God loves me, He does not keep score of all my sins and then beat me over the head with them whenever He gets the chance.
- Because God loves me He is deeply grieved when I do not walk in the ways that please Him because He sees this as evidence that I don't trust Him and love Him as I should.
- Because God loves me He rejoices when I experience His power and strength and stand up under the pressures of life for His Name's sake.
- Because God loves me He keeps on working patiently with me even when I feel like giving up and can't see why He doesn't give up with me, too.
- Because God loves me He keeps on trusting me when at times I don't even trust myself.
- Because God loves me He never says there is no hope for you, rather, He patiently works with me, loves me and disciplines me in such a way that it is hard for me to understand the depth of His concern for me.
- Because God loves me He never forsakes me even though many of my friends might.
- Because God loves me He stands with me when I have reached the rock bottom of despair, when I see the real me and

compare that with His righteousness, holiness, beauty and love. It is at a moment like this that I can really believe that God loves me.

Yes, the greatest of all gifts is God's perfect love!

(Dick Dickinson, Inter Community Counseling Center, Long Beach, California)

HELPING THE DEPRESSED PERSON

What should I do when a family member is depressed? What should I say? What shouldn't I say?

These are important questions. Most people don't know what to do for a depressed person. Here are some practical guidelines to follow. How closely you follow these will depend upon the intensity and duration of the person's depression. If he is depressed only for a few hours or for a day or two; if he is feeling down, but is functioning, not all of the suggestions would apply. But if the depression has lasted for quite a while; if he is dragging around, not functioning, not eating, not sleeping, you would want to apply the appropriate measures.

1. Understanding the causes and symptoms of depression is the first step toward helping. If your spouse is so depressed that he just stares or ignores greetings, or turns away from you, remember that he doesn't want to act this way. In depression, the person loses the ability to govern his thinking and his emotions. If he is severly depressed he cannot control himself any more than you could walk a straight line after twirling yourself around in a tight circle twenty-five times. If you understand how the person is feeling and why he is acting the way he is; if you understand that his behavior is the normal behavior of a depressed person; then you can be in better control of your own responses and you will be better able to help the depressed person.
2. Watch out for suicide: The family of a depressed person should be aware of this possibility. Any hint or statement or allusion to suicide should be talked about. It helps the depressed person to bring it out into the open and talk about it. Then he knows that others are aware and can be called upon to help and support. Ask him to tell you about his suicide thoughts or plans. Remember

too, that females make many more attempts than males, but males are more likely to succeed in taking their life. A divorced male over the age of forty is the highest risk. Any person who is so depressed that he talks about the utter hopelessness of the future might be considering suicide.

3. Get the depressed person to a doctor. Your family physician may be able to help or may recommend someone. The time factor is very important. Don't let depression go on and on. Even if the person keeps putting you off and refusing to go, make the arrangements, guide him firmly into the car, and go! We can't all use this next example, but one woman found it worked. Her husband, who ordinarily was very sociable and loved to be with others, sat around and moped or sat in front of the TV each evening. She insisted that he see a doctor, but he refused and said that nothing was wrong. Finally she gave him an ultimatum: "You go to the doctor in the next week or I will leave! I am not going to allow you to continue in pain!" This may be a last resort, but it motivated him to seek help. As long as you tolerate the other's depression, you

are helping to maintain it. The woman who pushed her husband to see a doctor was refusing to maintain his depression and to allow him to suffer. You may find your own creative but helpful way of encouraging your loved one to go for help.

If you are a wife with a depressed husband and you are not accustomed to taking charge, remember that your husband's illness makes it necessary to set aside your accustomed role in the marriage. Right now you are more capable of making the right decision and doing the right thing.

4. Give the person your full support. The entire family ought to be made aware of the situation and given instruction as to their responses. Confrontations with the depressed person should be suspended until he achieves greater stability. Tell them not to attack the depressed person, not to bring up his failures, not to come down hard on him, not to ask him to do things that he is not capable of doing while he is depressed.

5. Don't avoid the depressed person. This further isolates him and could make him worse. You might avoid him because you experience guilt over his depression

thinking that you may be the cause. Remember that one person may contribute to another's problem from time to time, but no one is responsible for another's unhappiness.
6. Understand that a depressed person really hurts. Don't suggest that he does not really feel badly or that he is just trying to get your sympathy. Don't tell him that all he has to do is "just pray about it and read the Word more" and that will solve everything. Often a depressed person chooses portions of the Scripture that reinforce his feelings of loss and unworthiness. Any Scriptures given to a depressed person must be selected with care. (See suggested Scriptures on p. 45.)
7. Empathize, rather than sympathize with your spouse. Sympathy can only reinforce a person's feelings of hopelessness. It may make him feel more helpless, and may lower his already low sense of self-esteem. Statements like, "It's so awful that you are depressed. You must feel miserable. How could this ever happen?" rarely help.
8. If your spouse is having difficulty sleeping, suggest a warm bath before going to bed; play some favorite music; or read an

interesting book to him. Your involvement shows that you care. If he suffers from severe insomnia it is helpful to sit up with him to convey to him that you care and that you are available and also to protect against any possible suicide attempts in severe cases. Eventually he will fall asleep, and you can get some sleep then too. If he doesn't want to eat you could say "Look, you may not feel like eating but you are probably hungry. Starving won't help. Food is important so let's eat now. I'll sit down and eat with you. And then let's talk about what's troubling you." Don't harp on the food problem or on his eating habits. If you say, "Oh, you'll make me feel badly if you don't eat this food," or, "Think of all the starving people," you won't get him to eat, but you could make him feel worse. Remember, not eating is a symptom of being depressed.

9. If your spouse or other family member loses interest in activities he normally enjoys, you can gently remind him of the past enjoyment that he derived from the activities and then firmly and positively insist that he become involved. Don't ask him if he would like to, as he might not know or may not care to

respond. Don't get angry and say, "You're going with me because I'm sick and tired of you sitting around feeling sorry for yourself." You could say, "I know that you have not felt well in the past, but I feel that you are entitled to some enjoyment. I think you might like this once we get started. And I would like to share this activity with you."

Or perhaps you call the theater to find out what time the concert begins. Upon hanging up you say to your spouse, "I think we can get ready for it, so let's start now." If you are going shopping you could suggest, "Come along. I like to have someone with me, and you know that I do rely upon your advice." Any activity such as window shopping, a social event or calling a friend can be used. By getting involved, the person begins to break the destructive behavior patterns, and this helps him gain energy and motivation.

One of the best things to do is to keep the person busy. Physical activity in severe depression can be more beneficial than mental activity. His entire day could be scheduled for him. The activities planned should be those that he or she has enjoyed in the past, with all preparations made in detail.

10. If your mate begins to let his or her appearance go, don't hint about the situation. Openly, clearly, and explicitly tell him that he will enjoy fixing himself up, and perhaps will feel better for it. You could go into his room, open the shades and windows for fresh air, help him get the room in order and lay out clean clothes.
11. Loss of confidence and self-esteem is common in depression. There are several steps to take in helping at this point. Don't ever kid or tease or lecture the person about his lack of confidence. And don't ignore it; it must be faced. In re-activating self-esteem, help the person see the illogic of his self-disparagement, but don't do it by berating or arguing. Look for *past accomplishments* in his life and get him to focus upon *what he was able to accomplish* prior to the onset of the depression. At this point you are trying to overcome his hopelessness. Don't join in the self pity, but respond by saying, "Perhaps you can't do anything the way you did before, but let's talk about the things you still do well. What do you think they are?" If he says, 'I can't do anything," gently name some things he can do, or draw them out of

him. Be persistent and steady in your responses. Remember that at this point you have more control of your emotional responses than he does.

By following these principles, it is possible for us to fulfill the biblical teaching of empathy and encouragement to one another. Galatians 6:1 says, "Brethren, if any person is overtaken in misconduct or sin of any sort, you who are spiritual—who are responsive to and controlled by the Spirit—should set him right and restore and reinstate him, without any sense of superiority and with all gentleness, keeping an attentive eye on yourself, lest you should be tempted also." Also I Thessalonians 5:14: "And we earnestly beseech you, brethren, admonish those who are out of line—the loafers, the disorderly and the unruly; encourage the timid and fainthearted, help and give you support to the weak souls (and) be very patient with everybody—always keeping your temper."

For Further Reading and Study
The Sensation of Being Somebody by Dr. Maurice Wagner, Zondervan Books. This book presents some excellent biblical and psychological teaching on self-concept.

Do I Have to Be Me by Lloyd Ahlem, Regal Books. The work contains helpful material on adequacy and self-concept.

The Christian Use of Emotional Power by H. Norman Wright, Revell. This book presents the thought life of a person as the basis for our emotional responses and deals with self-concept, anger, worry, and depression.

The Secret Strength of Depression by Fredrick Flach, Lippincott. One of the most helpful secular books on the subject.

Overcoming Depression and *Overcoming Frustration and Anger* by Paul Hauck, Westminster Publishers. Both volumes focus on the thought life of an individual as the key element in anger and depression.

Help for the Depressed by Samuel Kraine. This is a complete discussion of endogenous or biochemical depression, Thomas Publishers.

Up From Depression by Leonard Cammer, Pocket Books.

STUDY AND DISCUSSION IDEAS

1. Think back over your own life and list the times that you have been depressed. Try to determine the exact cause for the depression. You may want to re-read the section on causes of depression and then make your decision.
2. If you are reading or studying this with another person, tell him or her what helps you overcome times of depression or times of discouragement.
3. List ten passages from the Bible which you feel would help you the most in case of depression. Then select some passages that you might not want to share with depressed persons because they might misinterpret them or take them out of context.
4. Read through the first chapter of James. How would you apply James 1:2, "Consider it wholly joyful, my brethren, whenever you are enveloped in or encounter trials of any sort, or fall into various temptations.", to the problem of depression? Do you think it would help or hurt to share this passage with a depressed person?
5. Can experiences of sorrow prepare for and enlarge a person's capacity for joy?

How? (John 16:20; Romans 5:3, 4; II Cor. 7:4; 8:2).
6. During this next week make a graph or listing of the types of thoughts you have. Every time you experience a positive thought jot it down and give an indication as to how you felt. Do the same for the negative thought. If you find that you have more negative thoughts than you wanted, try out some of the suggestions given in this book. Keep checking to note improvement.
7. Discuss these questions and read this book together as a family. Share your reactions and develop a plan to help and encourage one another.